Mastering Effective Influencing Skills for Win-Win Outcomes

A practical guide

Mastering Effective Influencing Skills for Win-Win Outcomes

A practical guide

SARAH COOK

IT Governance Publishing

IT Governance Publishing Ltd
Unit 3, Clive Court
Bartholomew's Walk
Cambridgeshire Business Park
Ely, Cambridgeshire
CB7 4EA
United Kingdom
www.itgovernancepublishing.co.uk

© Sarah Cook 2024

The author has asserted the rights of the author under the Copyright, Designs and Patents Act, 1988, to be identified as the author of this work.

First published in the United Kingdom in 2024 by IT Governance Publishing.

ISBN 978-1-78778-537-3

Cover image originally sourced from Vecteezy.

PREFACE

This book is a practical guide to help equip you with the skills and confidence to effectively influence and persuade others in a variety of situations at work.

Influencing is an essential skill in many settings: building successful working relationships, effective communication, negotiations, getting one's ideas heard and successful networking. It is a soft skill that is applicable to leaders and managers as well as project managers and team members.

The guide will help you to understand what effective influencing is, to recognise the different styles of influence and the impact you have on others, and what your own and others' sources of power are and how to use these to influence others. It provides influencing strategies, tools and techniques that you can apply to the work environment and elsewhere.

The style of this book is very practical. It contains case study examples of successful influencing and persuading in different industries including the cyber security sector.

The guide contains advice, exercises, activities and diagnostics; all designed to help you improve your influencing skills.

I hope you enjoy the book and gain lots from it.

Sarah Cook, Managing Director, The Stairway Consultancy Ltd _www.thestairway.co.uk_

ABOUT THE AUTHOR

Sarah Cook is the Managing Director of The Stairway Consultancy Ltd. She has more than 20 years' consulting experience, specialising in leadership and management development. Before this, she worked for Unilever and as head of customer care for a retail marketing consultancy.

Sarah has practical experience in helping managers and team members develop their influencing skills at work. She works as an executive coach to help individuals to effectively create a positive impact.

As a business author, Sarah has written widely on leadership, career and management development, team building and coaching.

Sarah is a Chartered Fellow of the Chartered Institute of Personnel and Development and a Chartered Marketer. She has an MA from the University of Cambridge and an MBA from The Open University. Sarah is an accredited user of a wide range of psychometric and team diagnostic tools.

For more information about The Stairway Consultancy, please see _www.thestairway.co.uk_ or contact _sarah@thestairway.co.uk_.

Learn more about Sarah's other publications by visiting: _www.itgovernancepublishing.co.uk/author/sarah-cook_.

ACKNOWLEDGEMENTS

This book is based on best practice around positive influence and persuasion at work. The following organisations were valuable sources of reference:

Chartered Institute of Personnel and Development: *www.cipd.co.uk*

Chartered Management Institute

www.managers.org.uk

I would also like to thank the following reviewers for their helpful feedback during the production of this book:

- Vicki Utting – managing executive at IT Governance Publishing.
- Rosanna Allen – head of client services at IT Governance Ltd.

DISCLAIMER

All names quoted in this book are fictitious and have been presented for learning, understanding and explaining purposes only.

CONTENTS

Contents

CHAPTER 1: WHY INFLUENCING MATTERS

Introduction to influencing skills

Carol works in IT and is a subject matter expert in cyber security. She has been tasked with presenting a case for developing an insider risk management programme to the senior leadership team. Carol is very uneasy about making the presentation as she doubts her ability to persuade C-suite executives of the business case for the investment.

Although this situation may not have direct parallels with your own, as leaders, managers, team members, project leaders, consultants or contractors in the workplace, whatever role we play, we all need to be able to effectively influence and persuade others to arrive at win-win situations.

I suspect you are reading this book to improve your skills and confidence in influencing others. My intention is to provide you with practical advice and help you achieve this.

Influencing in its many forms at work

What does it mean to influence someone to do something? There are many definitions of 'influencing':

> *"The action or process of producing effects on the actions, behaviours, opinions, etc., of another or others."*[1]

> *"To affect or change how someone or something develops, behaves, or thinks."*[2]

> *"The capacity or power of persons or things to be a compelling force on or produce effects on the actions, behavior, opinions, etc., of others"*[3]

In an organisational context, we need to be able to influence well in a multitude of situations. These can include, among others:

- Networking and developing good interpersonal relationships;
- Leading and inspiring others;
- Communicating and gaining buy-in for our ideas;
- Promoting change;
- Developing a high-performing team; and
- Negotiating with others.

Influence or manipulation?

As an executive coach, quite often I'm asked, "Isn't influencing just a form of manipulation?"

---

[1] *https://www.dictionary.com/browse/influence*.

[2] *https://dictionary.cambridge.org/dictionary/english/influence*.

[3] *https://www.dictionary.com/browse/influence*.

Influence involves motivating people to work together to achieve a 'win-win' – the optimum outcome for a situation or organisation – without using force or coercion. It's based on the premise of respect, trust and building long-term relationships. The intention and the impact of influencing are positive.

Manipulation is a negative form of influence where someone seeks to create an imbalance of power that gives them the advantage; it's a 'win-lose' approach. The manipulator uses psychological or emotional tactics to get what *they* want. The intention and the impact of manipulation are negative. If you feel you have made a decision against your will, you are less likely to want to work with the person again; respect, trust and long-term relationships are eroded.

The focus of this book, therefore, is how to influence others with integrity and with the intention geared towards establishing credibility, building trust, and adding value to ongoing relationships.

Overview of the SOS model for developing your influencing skills

This book provides you with a toolkit to help you become more effective at work. In it, you'll find exercises and activities to help increase your influencing skills.

I will also take you through a model I've called 'SOS'. This stands for Self, Others, Strategy.

S = Self

The first step in developing your ability to influence effectively is to become more self-aware. This involves understanding your own influence and personal communication styles and the impact these have on others.

It also means being clear about the outcomes you desire from the situation where you need to influence others.

In the next chapters, you'll find explanations and self-assessment activities to help you develop your self-awareness.

O = Others

People who are successful at influencing put themselves in the shoes of the person or people they wish to influence. They prepare well to better understand the other person's goals and desired outcomes, what their preferred communication style is as well as their sources of power. By adopting techniques to help you better understand others, you'll be more aware of how to influence them.

S = Strategies

By understanding your own influencing style and recognising the communication preferences and power sources of others, you'll be better able to flex your own style to become more influential. You'll also be able to prepare strategies to better influence other people. In the last chapters of the book, I provide practical advice and examples on strategies you can adopt to achieve a win-win outcome in influencing others as well as advice on how to manage difficult situations.

Preparation for this book

To make this book as practical as possible, please select a situation (either current or in the past) where you would like /would have liked to influence others more effectively.

Please note:

- What is/was the situation?
- What is /was your desired outcome?
- Who else is/was involved?
- What is/was their perception of the situation?

I'll ask you to refer to this example at the end of the book. By the final chapter, you will have developed strategies related to this situation to help you (or that would have helped you) arrive at a successful outcome.

CHAPTER 2: RECOGNISING YOUR PERSONAL STYLE OF INFLUENCE

In this chapter, we discuss the importance of understanding your own influencing style, so you are more aware of what to do to best influence others. The chapter outlines:

- The difference between intention and impact;
- The different styles of communication and influence including a self-assessment of your current influencing style; and
- Practical tips for gaining feedback on your personal impact at work.

Intention versus impact

The main reason that Carol, the cyber security expert who is to make a presentation to the senior leadership team, lacks confidence in influencing this group is the feedback she received from her manager.

On the last occasion Carol presented to this team, her manager was also at the meeting. He told her afterwards that during the presentation, she gave too much detail, was hesitant, did not get directly to the point, and failed to convince the people she was trying to influence.

This feedback came as a blow to Carol as her intention had been to make an impactful presentation.

So, how can we influence others effectively? Our toolkit consists of our own actions and behaviours.

Intention

Actions and behaviours

What we say or do, and how we say or do it

Impact

Figure 1: Intention Versus Impact

When we fail to influence others effectively, it is usually not our intention to do so. Intention is what we mean to do – how we intend to act or behave. Impact is the result of what we do – the impact our action or behaviour has on others.

To influence effectively, we first need an awareness of how our own behaviour impacts others. In other words, what is our own personality style and what is its impact? How do we need to flex our style to influence others effectively?

Different personality types

Studies show that we can group people into one of four main types of personalities:

- Driver
- Analytical
- Amiable
- Expressive

Each personality type has a different style. Here is a description of each style:

	DRIVER	EXPRESSIVE
+ **O** **p** **e** **n** **n** **e** **s** **s** **O** **f** **C** **o** **m** **m** **u** **n** **i** **c** **a** **t** **i** **o** **n** **-**	Likes control. Takes charge. Focuses on the big picture. Likes competition. Takes risks. Believes that conflict can be constructive.	Has a lot of energy and Enthusiasm. Loves generating new ideas. Open to change. Is spontaneous. Recognises and praises the accomplishments of others. Has good persuasive skills.
	ANALYTICAL	**AMIABLE**
	Pays attention to detail. Thinks critically and analytically. Takes decisions based on facts. Has strong organisational skills. Sets high standards. Is disciplined, calm and rational.	Works cohesively with others. Is patient. Offers help when needed. Is considerate. Mediates conflict. Encourages others to share their feelings.

Displays Emotion

-   +

Figure 2: Description of the Four Personality Styles

On the Y axis is the degree of openness the person displays in communicating. People who are open in their communication, such as Drivers and Expressives, communicate freely; they tend to 'tell' rather than 'ask' and speak their mind openly.

People with personality types Analytical and Amiable are more closed and guarded in their communication style.

They are more likely to listen and ask questions than Drivers and Expressives.

On the X axis is the degree of emotion a person displays. Those with personality types Expressive and Amiable show their emotions both through what they say (e.g. they speak more freely about their feelings in comparison to Drivers and Analyticals). They also display more freely their feelings through their facial expressions (e.g. smiling, frowning, etc.), and body language (for example, they're more likely to touch and/or move close to others).

Drivers' and Analyticals' verbal communication focuses on facts rather than emotions. In terms of body language, they tend to have more 'dead pan' facial expressions and be more controlled in their body language.

Communication preferences per personality style

Each personality style also has different preferences for how they communicate, as shown below:

OPENNESS OF COMMUNICATION +

DRIVER	EXPRESSIVE
Gets to the point quickly and concisely. Freely shares opinions, is candid. Asks tough questions and raises difficult issues.	Energetic and passionate. Persuasive and engaging. Enjoys socialising before taking care of business.
ANALYTICAL	**AMIABLE**
Conversations are precise and to the point. Prefers to discuss facts not feelings. Takes care of business before Socialising.	Good listener. Builds trust. Uses supportive language e.g. 'I understand', 'I see'.

DISPLAYS EMOTION

-                                   +

Figure 3: Communication Preferences Per Personality Style

Take a moment to consider some examples of people with different personality styles in your own work environment or in the public eye.

- An example of a Driver is:
- An example of an Analytical is:
- An example of an Amiable is:
- An example of an Expressive is:

What is your own personality style?

Use the following questionnaire to see what your own preferences are.

Below, you'll find pairs of different adjectives. For each pair, consider how much they each describe you. Then assign a total of ten points between the two adjectives. Use any combination that adds up to ten, for example:

10 – 0
9 – 1
2 – 8
3 – 7
6 – 4
5 – 5

Table 1: Personality-style Questionnaire

Methodical AN ____	Energising E ____
Patient A ____	Spontaneous E ____
Results-focused D ____	Persuasive E ____
Talkative E ____	Likes to challenge people D ____

Detail-conscious AN _____	Forceful D _____
Strong-willed D _____	Generous A _____
Challenging D _____	Systematic AN _____
Consistent AN _____	Cooperative A _____
Efficient AN _____	Energising E _____
Accommodating A _____	Thorough AN _____
Supportive A _____	Lively E _____
Competitive D _____	Sympathetic A _____
Popular E _____	Decisive D _____

High-spirited E ____	Orderly AN ____
Encouraging to others A ____	Optimistic A ____
Accommodating A ____	Competitive D ____
Quickly gets to the point D ____	Supportive A ____
Analytical AN ____	Takes charge D ____
Logical AN ____	Patient A ____
Cautious AN ____	Results-oriented D ____
Enthusiastic E ____	Appreciative A ____

Analysing your results

Underneath each adjective in the table below, you will see the initials 'AN', 'D', 'E' or 'A'. Transfer your scores for each initial in to the boxes. Then total each column.

Table 2: Personality-style Scores

AN = Analytical	D = Driver	E = Expressive	A = Amiable
TOTAL Analytical	TOTAL Driver	TOTAL Expressive	TOTAL Amiable

Look which style has your highest score. This is the style that you use the most. (If your score is 75 or over, your style is very evident to others).

Also look at the style where you score lowest. This indicates the style you use least and where you'll probably have the least impact when you influence.

If you have two high scores (scores within eight points of each other), you probably use a combination of two different styles. These can be:

- Direct/Expressive;
- Direct/Systematic; or
- Amiable/Analytical.

(It is not possible to be Direct and Amiable, or Systematic and Expressive as opposites do not attract!)

The impact of different personality styles on others

When it comes to influencing others, if the person you are interacting with has a different personality style to your own, you may need to adapt your style of influence.

We tend to see the world through our lens or style. For example, other personality styles may see Drivers as putting results ahead of feelings, being overly critical and impatient and at times aggressive.

People who are not Expressives may see them as tending to exaggerate, being blindly enthusiastic and unrealistic and undisciplined.

People with other personality styles may see Analyticals as rigid and inflexible, reluctant to change, being too much of a perfectionist.

For Amiables, other people who do not have this style may see them as reluctant to express an opinion, too trusting, overly sensitive and staying too much in their comfort zone.

In our example, Carol, the cyber security expert, identified her personality style as Analytical.

When she considered the four directors she needed to influence, she realised that three of them were Drivers and one of them was Expressive.

Carol then understood how she needed to adapt her own style to better influence the leadership team.

Flexing your style

The first step in influencing others, therefore, is to recognise your own style and the style of the person/s you wish to influence.

Next, consider how you can flex your style to appeal to theirs.

For example, if you are an Expressive and wish to influence someone with a Direct personality style, you'll be wise to:

- Highlight the benefits of your ideas – provide a cost/benefit analysis;
- Keep it short and sweet;

- Be authoritative, avoid flippant remarks; and
- Expect and prepare for challenge.

If you wish to influence an Analytical:

- Provide facts and details, prior examples and evidence;
- Slow down your communication style;
- Allow time for reflection and don't expect a decision straight way; and
- Be rational, curb your enthusiasm.

If you're an Expressive and wish to influence an Amiable:

- Take time to establish a relationship;
- Highlight the benefits to everyone;
- Remember to be consultative and inclusive; and
- Be friendly and patient.

Likewise, if your personality style is not Expressive but you want to influence someone who is an Expressive:

- Take time to socialise before focusing on the facts;
- Stick to the big picture rather than the detail;
- Provide vivid examples; and
- Ask for their ideas.

Tips for gaining feedback on your personal impact at work

The questionnaire you have completed will help you assess your personality style. It is useful also to gain feedback from others at work about the impact you have when influencing and persuading Ask for feedback about what you do well and also how you can improve.

You can do this in several ways, such as:

- Asking for feedback directly from your manager, peers, team members and customers;
- Having a mentor at work who can provide you with feedback;
- Using 360-degree feedback surveys to identify your impact; and
- Attending influencing and other training workshops where you receive feedback from facilitators and coaches.

Takeaways from this chapter

1. You need to better understand your own personality style before you can better influence others .
2. There are four main personality type: Driver, Analytical, Amiable and Expressive. You may need to adapt your own style of communication to better appeal to the style of the person you are trying to influence.
3. Gaining feedback from others on how you currently influence is an important starting point.

CHAPTER 3: THE PUSH AND PULL MODEL OF INFLUENCING

In this chapter you'll find out more about:

- The Push/Pull model of communication;
- How your words, tone and body language need to be congruent;
- What your own communication preferences are; and
- How to recognise the communication preferences of others.

Congruent communication

As we've seen in the last chapter, we need to understand our own personality style and that of the people we wish to influence and adapt to these.

To have the impact we desire, our words, tone and body language need to be congruent and work in harmony. If our impact proves to be different from our intention, it is likely that our actions and words were mismatched thereby creating mixed messages to others.

> Carol wants to persuade the senior leadership team to agree to her idea, but when she discusses this with them, she subconsciously fails to make eye contact, rubs her neck nervously and speaks softly. Her body language and tone of voice therefore do not match the strong words she is using to put her case. The team picks up that she is not confident in putting forward her case.

When seeking feedback about your impact, remember to ask about what your body language and tone of voice says about you.

Communication styles

In terms of words, we can persuade others by the degree to which:

a) We are open and direct about what we need, want, expect and feel; and

b) How much consideration we show to others for their feelings, thoughts and opinions.

There are four main styles of communication that we can use with others:

Table 3: The Four Communication Styles

Openly aggressive behaviour	Direct and open about one's own thoughts and opinions but considers others' needs, thoughts or feelings very little. This behaviour may be described as domineering, pushy or self-centred.
Passive-aggressive behaviour	Not direct. Uses subtle ways, hints, sarcasm and jokes to convey one's thoughts and feelings to others. Displays little consideration for others' thoughts and feelings. This behaviour is often perceived as manipulative.

Passive behaviour	Reluctant to directly communicate own one's needs, thoughts or feelings to satisfy the needs and feelings of others. This behaviour breeds low self-esteem, frustration and withdrawal.
Assertive behaviour	Displays both openness and consideration for oneself and others. This behaviour allows an individual to communicate their thoughts and feelings in a way that is considerate and does not violate the rights of others.

Assertiveness

The most effective form of influencing is assertiveness. This is because it puts equal weight on what you want as on the wants and needs of the other person.

Yet being assertive is not an easy choice. Instinctively, when we face what we perceive to be a difficult or threatening situation, we adopt an emotional, irrational approach. Our inner defence mechanisms tell us to fight, flee or freeze. In difficult situations, we may, without thinking, become aggressive, or we may be passive or adopt a passive-aggressive approach. All these behaviours lead to an outcome where one person wins at the expense of the other or neither party achieves their desired outcome.

Assertiveness is a rational approach based on choice and is a learned behaviour. In a difficult situation, it involves taking a moment to pause, think, and not be driven by emotions.

Push and Pull behaviours

To influence assertively, you need to be able to say what you feel, think and need while at the same time respecting and valuing the views and opinions of others.

To do this, you need to be aware of when you use 'Push' behaviours and their counterpart, 'Pull' behaviours.

Push behaviours

Push behaviours are focused on expressing your own thoughts, needs and feelings. They include the following:

- **Proposing** – giving your own views and opinions, making proposals.
- **Directing** – stating what you need and expect of others.
- **Evaluating** – the ideas and opinions given to you by others.
- **Incentivising** – providing incentives to do something or stating the consequences of not doing something.

People who use predominantly Push behaviour work from their own agenda. They can be viewed by others as forceful, pushy or aggressive. Their language is very much centred on 'I', for example 'I want', 'I need'. The impact of their behaviour is that they signal that they want the other person to change.

The consequence of using too much Push can be that people on the receiving end become disenfranchised. They do not consider that their opinions are sought or valued. In the extreme, a Push style can appear dictatorial. People can lose respect for the person 'pushing' their opinions and this does not foster long-term relationships.

A further extension of Push behaviour is manipulation – using sarcasm, jokes, withdrawing from dialogue with the other person, demonstrating through your body language and/or tone that you are not happy.

This is a form of passive-aggression, sometimes called concealed aggression. The impact of this behaviour is that nothing is explicitly expressed, rather it's implied. An 'atmosphere' is created that is difficult to overcome.

Communication styles

	Aggressive	Assertive
HIGH **O** **p** **e** **n** **n** **e** **s** **s** LOW	**WIN** LOSE Passive- aggressive **LOSE** LOSE	**WIN** WIN Passive **LOSE** WIN

LOW   **Concern for others**   HIGH

Figure 4: The Outcomes of Different Communication Styles

Pull behaviours

Pull behaviours focus more on the other person. They include the following:

- **Enquiring** – asking questions to find out more from the person.

- **Listening and pacing** – actively listening, summarising. Matching the pace of the other person, going with their flow.
- **Being open to suggestions and ideas** – being open to other ways of doing things and being ready to change your mind.

These Pull behaviours focus on the other person. They show an interest in and consideration for the individual.

A further Pull behaviour focuses on 'we':

- **Finding areas of agreement** – building common ground, saying 'yes and' rather than 'yes but'.

The impact of using a Pull style of influence is to signal that you are prepared to change. You are working from the other person's agenda.

However, if you adopt a predominantly Pull style of influence all the time, you may be perceived as 'a walk over' or a passive person. You put other people's needs before your own. This style of influence can lead others to ignore and not to respect you and to diminishing self-confidence.

To influence effectively, therefore, we need to carefully consider how to adopt a style where we appropriately both Push and Pull.

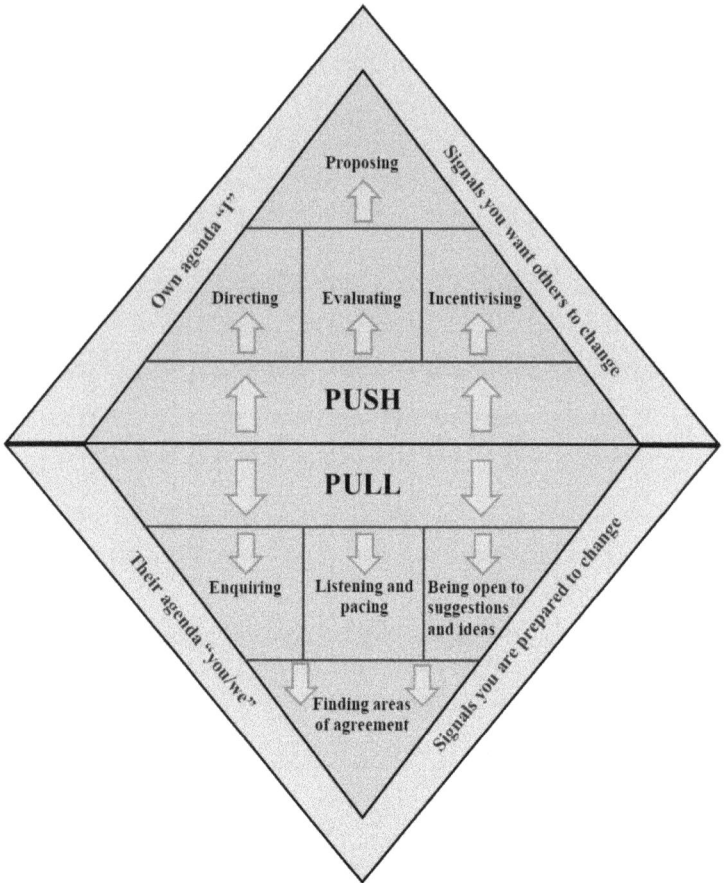

Figure 5: The Push-Pull Influencing Behaviours

To quote a famous saying of American philanthropist Andrew Carnegie;

> *"You cannot push anyone up a ladder unless he is willing to climb a little himself."*

Recognising when you to use Push or Pull

The first step in creating a win-win situation is clearly to recognise when you Push and when you Pull.

Push-Pull quiz

How well do you recognise Push and Pull behaviours?

Look at the expressions below and decide whether they are Push or Pull, then place an 'X' in the appropriate box:

Table 4: Push and Pull Quiz

Phrase:	Push	Pull
You must go and see him.		
So, you've said this is the most important aspect for you.		
What do you think about this?		
I think it's a great idea.		
I think we should change our plans.		
I can understand now why you're suggesting that.		
So, we all agree that…		

Phrase:	Push	Pull
If you complete it today, we'll all be able to leave on time.		

You'll find the answers to the quiz at the end of this chapter.

Which is your preferred style?

Do you use Push and Pull behaviours in equal measures? Use the following questionnaire to determine what your preferred style is.

Look at the following pairs of statements and for each one, decide which statement you agree with more. Tick the appropriate box (A or B) to show your agreement.

I mostly:

Table 5: Which is your Preferred Style?

A	B
Make suggestions and plans.	Develop other people's suggestions and plans.
Tell people the consequences of not doing something.	Find areas of common ground.

A	B
Point out the good and bad points about others' ideas.	Listen and give others a chance to explain their opinions.
Believe that my suggestions and ideas are the best.	Believe that others' suggestions and ideas are better than mine.
Tell people what they need to do.	Ask questions to see what the best course of action is.

Now total up the number of times you chose A and the number of times you chose B.

Understanding your results

Mostly As

You have a tendency to use Push behaviours rather than Pull. You believe that your ideas are better than others and you tend to push your opinions forward. This could be in a thoughtful way, although if you push too strongly, people will see you as aggressive.

Mostly Bs

You tend to use Pull behaviours rather than Push. You listen and ask questions to help you understand rather than expressing your own opinions. You like working in a team but may be overlooked as other people may see you as passive.

Equal As and Bs

You use a mixture of Push and Pull behaviour. This means you can express your ideas and opinions in a direct way at the same time as listening and building on the ideas of others. Your mix of Push and Pull behaviours indicates that you can flex your style in an assertive manner.

Getting feedback on how you Push and Pull

The brief questionnaire above reflects your own self-perception. It's important to gather feedback from other people too about the degree to which you Push and Pull; what impact your body language and tone have, and whether people see you as assertive, passive, aggressive or passive-aggressive.

Using both Push and Pull

In most influence situations, we need to use both Push and Pull to persuade others and arrive at a win-win outcome.

For example, if you are trying to influence a team member to adopt a new approach, you may say:

"What do you think about the proposed new ways of working?" (Pull – enquiring.)

"So, from what you're saying, you believe..." (Pull – listening and pacing.)

"I suggest that we take some time to embed the changes..." (Push – proposing.)

> *"The one area I need you to focus on now is..."* (Push – directing.)

Flexing your style

Over time, we build up patterns of behaviour that we adopt without even thinking about them. If you wish to influence better, you may need to be able to use both Push and Pull and to flex your style according to the situation. Here are two examples:

Pierre is a line manager who is viewed by his team as very direct. He likes to take charge and frequently expresses his views and ideas in meetings. His style is seen as quite pushy by some, and he is constantly telling his team members what to do.

In the past eighteen months, Pierre has lost three direct reports in his team. The feedback that he's received from HR is that his Push communication style does not influence team members to stay.

Having worked with a coach, Pierre realised that he needed to ask more questions to engage his team members more as well as being more open to their suggestions.

By addressing the balance of Push and Pull, Pierre hopes to influence more effectively.

Alex is an IT consultant and is used to working by herself. As a result of organisational changes, she now finds herself in a new department where she is a subject matter expert.

Alex is a good listener and likes working in a team. She is more comfortable building on other people's ideas, rather than expressing her own.

Alex has received feedback from her manager that she is too passive in meetings and makes little contribution although she has a great deal of knowledge to share.

Alex has set herself the goal of making more proposals and suggestions in meetings. To do this, she is working on building her confidence and improving her body language.

In the example we are using of Carol, the cyber security expert, she too recognised that she needed to be more confident, direct and less passive when interacting with senior leaders. In chapter 5, I'll share some tips on how she did this.

Takeaways from this chapter

1. The words we use, our tone and our body language create an impact on others.
2. They also convey a message to others about whether we are assertive, aggressive, passive or passive-aggressive.
3. To influence effectively, we need to use a mixture of both Push and Pull behaviours.

4. Push behaviours – proposing, directing, evaluating and incentivising; and Pull behaviours – enquiring, listening, being open to suggestions and finding agreement.

5. If your Push/Pull behaviours are out of balance, set yourself a target of improving one aspect of the Push/Pull behaviours you use less frequently to begin addressing this imbalance.

Table 6: Answers to Push/Pull Quiz

Phrase:	Push?	Pull?
You must go and see him.	X Directing	
So, you've said this is the most important aspect for you.		X Listening
What do you think about this?		X Enquiring
I think the idea I've proposed is a great one.	X Evaluating	
I think we should change our plans.	X Proposing	

Phrase:	Push?	Pull?
I can understand now why you're suggesting that.		X Being open to suggestions
So, we all agree that …		X Finding agreement
If you complete it today, we'll all be able to leave on time.	X Incentivising	

CHAPTER 4: DEVELOPING SELF-CONFIDENCE

Think of someone who has good persuasion skills and effectively influences others. Typically, these people have a high degree of self-confidence.

To influence well, we need to be seen as credible, convincing and trustworthy. To ensure that others find you believable, you need to believe in yourself.

In our last example, IT consultant Alex has set herself the goal of making more proposals and suggestions in meetings. She knows that Push is not her natural style and that she prefers to listen to others in meetings. Her issue is that she spends a long time formulating what she wants to say in her head before speaking. Often, she finds that the meeting has moved on and she has not expressed her opinions. Alex is also prone to comparing herself in a negative light to her colleagues. To influence more effectively, Alex recognises she needs to improve her self-confidence.

Carol, too, the cyber security expert, recognised that she needed to be more confident and less passive when interacting with senior leaders. With her colleagues and other peers she is more assertive.

Activities to develop self-confidence

If you, too, find you are sometimes lacking in self-confidence and this is impeding your ability to influence well, on the next pages are some practical activities to help.

a) Developing self-confidence

To help improve your confidence:

1. List your greatest strengths (e.g. loyalty, a sense of humour, good negotiating skills, friendliness, honesty).
2. Write down how these strengths have helped you in life.
3. How could you improve on these strengths?
4. How can you use them to help you achieve more of your goals at work, at home, or in contact with others?
5. Look back at your answers to question 1. Then, set a goal as to how you would like to feel about yourself. Write it down.
6. Write down the benefits of having more confidence in yourself.

Each evening, over the course of the week, record how these strengths have helped you in various situations during the day.

b) Create a positive letter of affirmation

Write a list of statements about you that you know are true – you need at least six statements.

Write them in the present tense using positive language, for example:

> *"I am a calm person and a logical thinker."*
>
> *"I am a confident speaker."*

> *"I am a great problem-solver."*

Keep this list of positive affirmations with you at work and read them twice a day for approximately three weeks.

After three weeks, you should be able to memorise these so you can say them to yourself during any stressful situation to alleviate your anxiety.

c) Avoid comparing yourself to others

People with low self-confidence tend to compare themselves to others and consider themselves less able, experienced or confident. They may have self-doubt and feel they are not worthy of their position, that soon they will be 'found out'. Sometimes called 'imposter syndrome', this can put their own happiness and well-being at risk.

To avoid this tendency, re-frame how you think about others. If you see someone who is good, for example, at speaking 'off-the-cuff' in meetings, think: 'What can I learn from this person?', rather than: 'I'll never be as good at doing that'.

Focus on the things that are going well in your life and that you are grateful for. This is a technique called a 'gratitude list'. It involves writing down every day one or two things that you appreciate. This can be anything that resonates with you, such as 'The view of the sunrise from my window this morning' or 'My sister sending me a WhatsApp to see how I am'. When you find your own contentment, you are less likely to compare yourself to others.

d) Confidence starts at home

If you lack self-confidence, you'll often find it hard at times to recognise your strengths and talk about your needs. This will probably be as much at home and with friends as it is with colleagues and your manager at work.

A safe place to begin building your confidence is by talking about your achievements with friends and family. Speak about small successes and things you are proud of; it doesn't have to be work related – the meal you have cooked and are pleased with or a good walk you have undertaken with friends. The importance is to find your voice and feel comfortable about articulating your contribution to something. The more you practice this at home, the easier it will become to speak up about your strengths in a work environment.

e) Visualise yourself being successful

The ability to see yourself doing things well acts as a programme for the mind to put those steps into action – the mind cannot differentiate between fact and fiction!

To visualise success, think of an occasion or situation where you do not feel confident, like presenting in front of a certain group of people.

Close your eyes and imagine yourself being successful. Watch yourself doing what you want to happen.

Consider:

- Where you are;
- Who is with you;
- What you are saying and doing;

- How you are looking – how you are dressed and the gestures you use; and
- The positive reactions from others to what you are saying and doing.

Play this 'tape' over several times in your mind, making the picture clearer and clearer each time. Notice the physiological changes as you do this and how much more positive you feel about the event.

It's especially helpful to play the tape over again in your mind just before any situation where you need to be confident.

f) Positive self-talk

This activity will help you become more aware of your emotions and self-talk in two contrasting situations: one where you are confident and the other where you lack confidence. In this way, you'll be more aware of the need for positive self-talk to be confident.

Firstly, think of an occasion recently where you have felt confident. Write down:

- What was happening?
- What were you saying to yourself about the situation (your self-talk)? What tone did your self-talk have? What kind of language were you using?
- What physical sensations and feelings were you aware of?

What was the outcome of the situation?

Next, think of an occasion recently where you have not felt confident. Write down:

- What was happening?
- What were you saying to yourself about the situation (your self-talk)? What tone did your self-talk have? What kind of language were you using?
- What physical sensations and feelings were you aware of?

What was the outcome of the situation?

Now compare your reactions to the two situations. Think about the actions you can take the next time you lack confidence and answer the following questions:

1. What positive statement could I say to myself to be reminded of my strengths and achievements?
2. What could I do that would help me feel differently?
3. What could I do differently next time I am in this situation?
4. What self-talk or actions would empower me?

Takeaways from this chapter

1. Self-confidence is an important element in persuading others.
2. Use the practical activities in this chapter to help you improve your confidence.

CHAPTER 5: IDENTIFYING SOURCES OF POWER

Carol recognised that part of her passive behaviour when interacting with senior leaders was driven by fear – the unspoken power the leaders had over Carol's long-term future at the company.

In this chapter, you'll learn more about how power sources offer a filter that helps us influence and work effectively with others. We can adapt our approach and communication when we notice the power sources used by others as follows:

- Knowing your own power sources can help you understand why you're able to influence.
- Recognising others' sources of power can help you develop strategies for influencing others.
- Although power sources can help us influence, they can be overplayed with negative consequences, and we'll also discuss these.

What power do you have to influence others at work?

In my own organisation, I've noticed that our marketing manager Osman has made friends with someone who works in IT. This means that when Osman has an IT issue, rather than go through the normal process (report the problem using the badge number, get a ticket, wait until, the help desk contacts him, have the issue resolved) – he can ask his friend in IT what he needs to do to resolve the issue.

This is an example of what is called 'referent power', the influence that you have when you are liked by others.

Power comes in many different forms, and we can increase our influence if we understand each type of power we can use to influence. Psychologists Bertram Raven and John French[4] identified and developed a framework for understanding five different types of power. Bertram Raven, Arie Kruglanski, and Paul Hersey, working with Marshall Goldsmith, expanded the original framework from five to seven types of power by adding 'connection' and 'information' powers.[5]

Identify your own sources of power

Use the following self-assessment questionnaire to identify your own power sources.

Consider each of the following statements and allocate a score on a scale of 1 (you do not agree at all with this statement) to 10 (you totally agree with this statement).

---

[4] French, J R P Jr and Raven, B (1959). "The bases of social power". In Cartwright D (Ed.), Studies in social power (pp 150–167). University of Michigan.

[5] Bertram Raven (1959) continued the research and collaborated with Arie Kruglanski, Paul Hersey and Marshall Goldsmith (Hersey and Blanchard, 1982).

You'll have a chance to score your questionnaire later in the chapter.

Others respond to my efforts to influence because:

Table 7: Power-sources Questionnaire

	YOUR SCORE
I have the power to administer sanctions to those who don't cooperate with me.	A __
I have connections with important people inside and/or outside the workplace.	B __
People respect my expertise, skill and knowledge.	C __
People believe that I have inside information that will be useful to them.	D __
People feel I have the right to tell them what to do due to my position in the organisation.	E __
I am generally liked and admired by others because of my personality.	F __
People believe that by doing what I want them to, they can gain positive	G __

incentives such as pay, promotion or recognition.	
I can induce compliance because failure to comply will lead to unfavourable consequences such as reprimands, warnings or dismissal.	A __
Others aim to gain the favour or avoid the disfavour of my important or influential connections.	B __
I am seen as having the expertise to facilitate the work of others.	C __
I have information or access to information that is perceived as valuable to others.	D __
My position within the organisation allows me to direct others' work activities.	E __
People like me personally and therefore do things that please me.	F __
I can provide reward to others who give me their support.	G __

The seven sources of power

Here is a description of the seven sources of power:

Table 8: Sources of Power

Coercive power: Based on fear. The person uses this power because failure to comply will lead to a disadvantage for the other person, such as undesirable work projects, reprimands, warnings or dismissal.

Connection power: Based on having connections with influential or important people inside or outside the organisation. Other people aim to gain the favour of this person (or avoid disfavour) and access to their powerful connection.

Expert power: Based on someone's expertise, skill and knowledge. They use this to gain the respect of others. Someone with expert power can facilitate the work of others.

Information power: Based on someone's possession of or access to information that is perceived as valuable to others. This influences others because they need this information or want to be 'in on things'.

Legitimate power: Usually applies to someone in a position of authority. The higher the position, the higher the legitimate power tends to be. Someone with legitimate power induces compliance from or influence over others because others feel that this person has the right by virtue of their position in the organisation.

Referent power: Based on someone's personal traits. This person is generally liked and admired by others because of their personality.

Reward power: Based on someone's ability to provide rewards for other people. Other people believe that their compliance will lead to gaining positive incentives such as pay, promotion or recognition.

Identifying power sources

Look at the table above and consider examples of people you know who demonstrate any of the different sources of power:

- Coercive power
- Connection power
- Expert power
- Information power
- Legitimate power
- Referent power
- Reward power

Your own sources of power

Now think about your own sources of power. Which of the seven sources resonate with you?

Scoring of your self-assessment questionnaire

Return to the questionnaire you completed earlier. Transfer your scores to the grid below:

Table 9: Scoring of Self-assessment Questionnaire

Total your score for each letter	Total score out of 20
A = Coercive power	
B = Connection power	
C = Expert power	
D = Information power	
E = Legitimate power	
F = Referent power	
G = Reward power	

Now look at your highest scoring sources of power. (If you have two or more sources of power that are high scoring, this means you use more than one source).

Consider: What do your scores tell you about how you currently influence others?

Advantages and disadvantages of each source of power

For each power source, there are things that can be helpful as well as drawbacks. For example:

Table 10: Advantages and Disadvantages of Each Power Source

Power sources	Advantages	Disadvantages
Coercive power	Good crisis management tool	People only respond to fear for so long, undermines position if it's relied on, so seen as weak
Connection power	Builds relationships quickly	Name-dropping can irritate some people
Expert power	Gets correct answers in short time	May stifle others' ideas
Information power	Can broaden discussions	Withholding can cause resentment
Legitimate power	Gets the job done quickly	Can be seen as pulling rank

Power sources	Advantages	Disadvantages
Referent power	Builds or increases trust, confidence and credibility in relationships	Can give the impression of being 'too nice' or false
Reward power	Can motivate people	Rewards become expected and need to get bigger

Be wary of overuse of certain power sources. Coercive, connection and reward power require more careful application because they rely upon a higher degree of trust and risk, and can easily become manipulative.

There is a strong relationship between credibility, influence and power. When it comes to influencing people without creating potentially negative effects, referent, expert, information and legitimate power tend to get the best results.

Appealing to other people's sources of power

We can adapt our approach and communication when we notice the power sources used by others.

Here are some suggestions about how to appeal to the different power sources of others:

Table 11: Appealing to Other People's Sources of Power

Coercive power	Be time critical.
Connection power	Ask them to introduce you to someone with whom they're connected. Introduce them to someone you know who could be helpful to them.
Expert power	Ask for their opinions. Refer to their expertise. Check what you have is correct before sending information to them.
Information power	Ask for and share relevant information.
Legitimate Power	Copy them into emails. Keep them informed. Get the final approval from them.

Referent power	Build relationships and teams through creating trust, have natural conversations, listen well.
Reward power	Develop project milestones. Celebrate success.

Using the information about sources of power, Carol realised that the four senior leaders used legitimate power to influence others and that she needed to 'play' to this power in the meeting. She also noticed that one of the leaders was well liked by all and used referent power to build alliances.

Carol's self-assessment showed that she in turn used expert and referent power at work.

She recognised that her expert power could be helpful in influencing the senior leadership team and that she should use this more strongly when making her case.

Takeaways from this chapter

1. There are seven sources of powers that we can use to influence others: coercive power, connection power, expert power, information power, legitimate power, referent power, reward power.

2. Referent, expert, information and legitimate power tend to get the best results in terms of influence.

3. It is useful to know your own sources of power as well as to identify those of others so that you can adapt your style appropriately.

CHAPTER 6: INFLUENCING STRATEGIES

In the previous chapters, we have spoken about the need to know our own personality and communication styles and sources of power as well as recognising the preferences and power sources of others.

In this chapter, we discuss:

- Trust and relationship building;
- How to get yourself heard; and
- Strategies for influencing and persuading others.

Trust is a key ingredient

Trust is a key ingredient in effective influencing and persuasion. It is built over time and involves earning a level of credibility with others so that they see you as dependable and predictable in how you act. It involves having confidence in the person you are dealing with.

To build trust, Harvard professors Maister, Green and Galford[6] identified that people need to be credible and 'know their stuff'. They need to be reliable and keep their promises, and they also need to establish long-term relationships. The professors pointed out that trust can be destroyed by self-orientation (self-interest), so engaging

---

[6] Maister, D; Green, C; Galford, R (2001). *The Trusted Advisor*. Simon & Schuster. New York.

with people for the common good and working to a common goal is important.

Getting heard

As we have already seen, being assertive is important for influencing well. The balance of Push and Pull behaviours, delivered in a congruent manner, helps promote a respectful and open environment.

When you want to get your point across assertively, you need to consciously use a mixture of Push and Pull techniques.

For example, imagine you want to influence your manager to provide you with external support to finish a project. He does not believe that you need additional resource.

You need to:

- ***Listen*** *actively to the other person; and*
- ***Acknowledge*** *what they say and feel, and why.*

In this situation, you could say to your manager: *"I appreciate that we need to finish the project by next week. I understand that you feel that we don't need additional resource because we have the knowledge in-house."*

- ***Pause***

Gain your manager's attention by pausing before you speak next. This also allows you to gather your thoughts.

- ***Win yourself a hearing***
  - *Say clearly what you feel and think.*
  - *Say specifically what you want to happen.*

o *Support what you are saying by how you say it.*

In our example, this would sound something like: *"We have a lot of other critical commitments in the same time frame that we need to achieve. I strongly believe we need additional resources to help complete this key project.*

"So, I whole-heartedly recommend that we look straight away at using an external consultant to help us do this."

- **Work to a joint solution**
  o *Aim for a win-win outcome.*

You could say: *"Would you agree for me to contact the consultant to see how much they might charge to help? We'll benefit from this in the long run as it will save us time and effort and ensure we meet all our commitments."*

Powerful words

You will notice that in the above example, I used what I call 'powerful words'. Adverbs or qualifiers that add emphasis to the points you are making.

'I feel *strongly.*'

'I *whole-heartedly* recommend.'

Powerful words, together with open and direct language, help influence others.

Influencing strategies

Consider, too, which is the best strategy to use in terms of your audience.

In chapter 2, we discussed the four personality styles: Amiable, Driver, Expressive and Analytical.

There are four influencing strategies that people can choose from to appeal to each personality style. Two of the strategies rely on facts to persuade others and the other two rely on emotions.

1. Logical facts

This strategy involves using logic to persuade people. It uses facts and figures in a structured and sequential manner.

If our expert Carol decides to use an 'Asserting Logical' strategy in presenting a case to the senior leadership team for developing an insider risk management programme, she may assertively say that "75% of the increase in average breach costs in this year's [IBM Cost of a Data Breach Report] was due to the cost of lost business and post-breach response activities." The report also highlights that 4.88 million USD is "the global average cost of a data breach in 2024 — a 10% increase over last year and the highest total ever."[7]

2. Pros and cons

This also uses a rational approach. People who adopt this strategy promote the benefits of their ideas and highlight

---

[7] *https://www.ibm.com/reports/data-breach.*

the weaknesses of the current situation. They are prepared to debate with others and they use logic to advance their proposals.

If Carol were to adopt a pros and cons approach, she may stress that the advantages of implementing an insider risk management programme is that clients and other stakeholders can be assured of secure and confidential transactions. Without it, the organisation can be vulnerable to data leakage, policy violations, intellectual property theft and compliance breaches.

Logical facts and pros and cons are strategies based on facts. There are two influencing strategies that draw on emotions:

3. Big picture

People who use a big-picture strategy paint a compelling vision of the future. They use motivating language to engage others via inspirational appeals, stories and metaphors to encourage a shared sense of purpose.

Carol might say, "Insider risk has the capacity to sink our ship. It's like navigating with radar in stormy waters and not seeing the icebergs in the dark."

4. Participative

This strategy entails involving other people in ideas and decision-making. This is a collaborative style that involves all members of the team.

Carol may say that she knows the senior leadership team have concerns about data leakage; she may then ask the board members what would be most important to them when developing an insider risk programme.

Which of the four options best suits which personality style?

Consider the four strategic options we've just discussed:

1. Logical facts.
2. Pros and cons.
3. Big picture.
4. Participative.

Now think of the four personality types: a) Amiables; b) Drivers; c) Analyticals; and d) Expressives. Consider which strategy appeals to which style. (See answers at the end of this chapter.)

How do you convince a group of people who have different styles?

The answer is to appeal to the dominant style of the group. For example, if you are trying to persuade a group of engineers about a new idea, chances are that their style will be Analytical, so an approach asserting facts in a logical way should appeal to the majority.

However, if you are asked a specific question from someone in the group who you identify as having a different personality style, be prepared to flex your style to this person.

Other tactics

In addition to the four strategic options, a variety of other techniques can be used to influence others, such as:

- Ingratiation;
- Exchange of benefits;
- Appealing to others; and
- Coalitions.

Ingratiation

As the name implies, this involves ingratiating yourself via such approaches as flattery, compliments and support. The aim is to appear a loyal and invaluable person in the eyes of the person whom you wish to influence. This is a passive-aggressive approach that does not build long-term relationships. The individual is trying to manipulate the other person via ingratiating themselves.

Exchange of benefits

Negotiating trade-offs is a tactic that some people use as a form of influence: 'I'll give you two people from my team to help you on the project if you provide me with the information I need for the report.'

Appealing to others

If you are having difficulty convincing someone or getting them on your side, upwards appeal can be exercised by appealing to the person's boss, colleague, or a subject matter expert such as an external consultant. In this way, you hope that the boss/colleague, etc. will influence them to come round to your way of thinking. However, a downside of this approach is that the person you are trying to influence may resent this and it can damage your long-term relationship with them.

Coalitions

Often used in organisations, forming coalitions involves aligning yourself with other people who share the same views as you. This tactic ensures that you will gain support from others in the face of opposition. Like appealing to others, ingratiation and exchange of benefits, however, a coalition strategy can be a covert tactic and, as such, it can cause suspicion and mistrust.

> In Carol's situation, she realised that as her audience were 'drivers', she needed to use a pros and cons strategy to present her case. She also noted that since one of the senior leaders, the HR director, used referent power to influence, she could potentially approach him to see if she could build a coalition with him about the insider risk programme.

Assess your use of influencing strategies

Thinking of a specific situation where you need to influence, look at the list below and tick those strategies you have already used to influence others. Tick those strategies that would be useful in the future:

Table 12: Strategies You Can Use

Strategy	Used already	Can use in future
Logical facts		
Pros and cons		
Big picture		
Participative		
Ingratiation		
Exchange of benefits		
Appealing to others		
Coalitions		

Takeaways from this chapter

1. Trust is central to developing long-term relationships.
2. Getting heard involves using both Pull and Push techniques in a congruent manner.
3. According to the personality style of the person you are trying to influence, you can use logical facts, pros and cons, big-picture or participative strategies. Other strategies include ingratiation, exchange of benefits, appealing to others and coalitions.

Answers to which strategy to use

a) **Amiables** – Participative.

b) **Drivers** – Pros and cons.

c) **Analyticals** – Logical facts.

d) **Expressives** – Big picture.

CHAPTER 7: DEALING WITH REACTIONS WHEN YOU PRESENT YOUR IDEAS

Have you ever been in a situation where you're trying to influence someone of the benefits of something, but their response indicates that they are cynical or that they may agree with you but they don't want to actively go along?

In this chapter, we assess the reactions that people have when faced with change, how to influence effectively and present a positive approach, as well as how to deal with people's reactions.

People's reactions to new ideas

Imagine that you have just presented an idea for a major change in a process that will impact the rest of your team. There are various reactions among the team that lead you to believe that you have not positively influenced enough people to implement the idea effectively.

The reactions you've seen are linked to two sets of behaviours:

- Their attitude towards new ideas and change, be it positive or negative.
- Their drive towards activity, be it active or inactive.

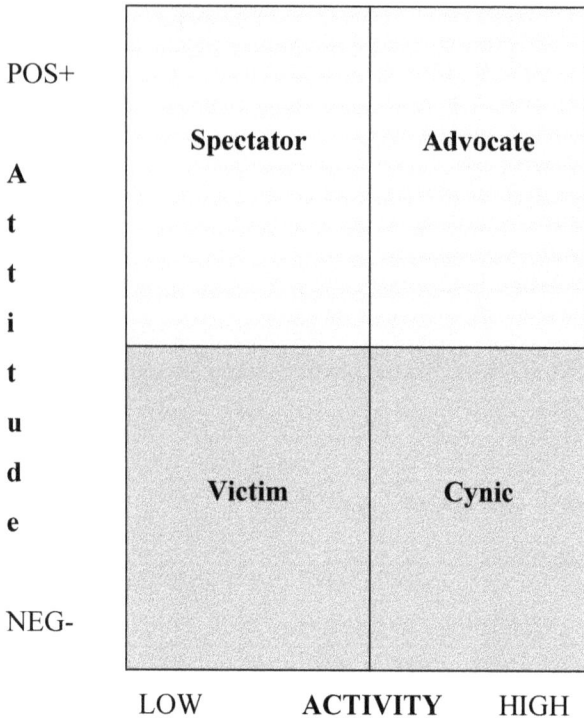

POS+	Spectator	Advocate
A t t i t u d e		
	Victim	Cynic
NEG-		
	LOW ACTIVITY HIGH	

Figure 6: The Attitude and Activity Model

The descriptions below will help you recognise each type:

Advocates: Have a positive attitude to change and are action-oriented. They are prepared to 'give it a go' and realistic about obstacles they encounter and how to overcome them. Advocates react to new ideas and change by:

- Seeing the silver lining hidden beneath the clouds;
- Viewing change as challenge and opportunity;

- Treating life as a continual learning experience; and
- Expanding their personal comfort zone.

Advocates tend to feel comfortable with the need for change, be open to new possibilities and ideas, be optimistic about the long-term future, enjoy being challenged and stretched, are realists and are not afraid of short-term mistakes or setbacks.

Cynics: Display a negative attitude. These people are highly active and vocal, telling others why new ideas they don't own won't work. They are keen to disassociate themselves from change.

Cynics actively criticise and express frustrations, focusing on the past – 'We tried this five years ago…'. They are often oblivious to the consequences of their negativity, bringing other people round to their perspective. They can feel not listened to and excluded but are overtly confident in their own ability and unsympathetic to the stress felt by others.

Spectators: Characterised by being positive towards new ideas but not following this through with action. They say the right things and agree to the change in principle but are inactive when it comes to doing something about it. They tend to avoid taking risks and like to keep a low profile, being comfortable to watch from the sidelines.

Victims: Have a negative attitude towards new ideas and change, and lack drive. They avoid and ignore the change for as long as possible. This inactivity coupled with their negative approach towards new ideas leads to inertia. Although less vocal than Cynics, they still disengage from new ideas and change; everything is 'done to them', they do not take an active part. They avoid confronting issues, bury their heads in the sand, feel powerless and fearful of mistakes.

Typical phrases used

Here's what you'd hear in response to your ideas from each type:

Advocate: *"I can", "I will"*.

Cynic: *"It won't work", "I can't support it"*.

Spectator: *"I would if I could"*.

Victim: *"I can't", "I won't be able to"*.

What is your backup style?

We can all demonstrate different behaviours at different times. Under pressure and with the stress that change frequently brings, people tend to revert to a 'backup' style. For example, I know I am an Advocate for most ideas. However, when I'm busy and have too much on, I can become a Spectator – saying all the right things but not following through. Spectator is my backup style.

Take a few minutes to look back at the model and the characteristics of each type. Identify your backup style during the last change that you experienced at work.

- What does this tell you about yourself during change?
- What reasons could there be for you to act in this way?

Think of an occasion when you demonstrated this style.

- What was the effect on the customer, your team or your colleagues?

Now consider people on your team and their reactions to a new idea or recent change. What was each team member's backup style during the change? Identify people who demonstrated each of the styles on the model.

Dealing with Cynics, Victims and Spectators

As we have seen, the style of influence that you use has a direct impact on the reactions of others during change.

When you present new ideas and have Cynics, Victims or Spectators in your audience, here are some actions you can take based on Push and Pull to encourage them to become Advocates:

Cynics

These are often experienced people who have been with the organisation for some time and have 'been round the block'. To become Advocates, Cynics need to:

- Talk less and listen more;
- Be aware of the negative impact they create;
- Voice their concerns in a more positive manner and criticise less; and
- Ask to take on challenges and make the most of them.

To convince a Cynic to adopt your ideas, initially adopt Pull tactics – ask them their views and opinions, listen and acknowledge these, and where possible, get them involved in implementing your ideas. Ensure you remain firm in the face of their opposition. Give them responsibility for making something work.

Spectators

To become Advocates, Spectators need to:

- Not over-promise when they can't deliver;
- If they cannot meet deadlines, enlist others' help;
- Follow things through to completion; and
- Be more confident in putting forward and acting on ideas.

To influence Spectators, it's best to adopt Push tactics – be clear about what you want and what needs to happen, set them targets and stretching goals. Monitor their progress and set them deadlines to ensure things get done.

Victims

To become Advocates, Victims need to:

- Be more confident in themselves;
- Ask for help if the task is too daunting;
- Consider the impact they are having on others;
- Play a more positive role in the team; and
- Consider what work they would really like to be doing, and do it.

To encourage a Victim to become an Advocate, start with a Pull approach to find out what they like or dislike about your ideas. Move to Push to set small challenges and to tell the person how you would like them to change their behaviour. Be prepared to have a lot of input with this person if you want them to continue in their current role.

Advocates

Do not forget to encourage and recognise Advocates, early adopters of your ideas. They too need a mixture of Push and Pull to help them do the following:

- Set a positive example;
- Put forward ideas for improvement;
- Encourage and support their fellow team members; and
- Tell their manager when Cynics, Spectators and Victims are having a negative impact.

Provide recognition and praise to this person and involve them in your implementation plans.

Carol recognises that one of the executives she will present to is very cynical when it comes to new ideas. He has a powerful influence over his peers and she needs his buy-in to start the project.

She realises that she will be challenged by him in the meeting and needs to prepare to listen to his concerns and look at ways of building his ideas into the programme.

Takeaways from this chapter

1. People's attitude and levels of activity vary when they listen to ideas that others present. They can be labelled as Advocates of your ideas, Cynics, Spectators or Victims.

2. To engage others in your ideas, you need to know how to manage each type, using a mixture of Push and Pull techniques to gain buy-in.

CHAPTER 8: NEGOTIATION SKILLS

In this chapter, we look at why negotiation skills are an important element of influencing, the different approaches you can take when you negotiate and their impact, as well as tips for successful negotiation.

> Carol has identified that she can potentially form a coalition with HR to gain support for the programme. She gains permission from her manager to meet with the HR director before her presentation to negotiate for his support.

There will undoubtedly be times when negotiation is called for. Baroness Karren Brady, the 'first lady of football', took up the role of managing director at Birmingham City Football Club in 1993 when she was 23, turning round a run-down club by changing the philosophy of the business. There will undoubtedly be times when negotiation is called for. People who are successful negotiators start by first deciding what they want and what they are willing to exchange for it. This is the fundamental principle of negotiation.

Negotiation is a useful influencing strategy, particularly when two groups have differing points of view.

When groups compete against each other, certain behaviours prevail:

- The other group is seen as the enemy.
- Each group closes ranks and become more tightly knit.

- Each group believes that they are better than the other – they focus on their own strengths but deny their own weaknesses, while doing the opposite with the opposing party.
- As hostility increases, there is a reluctance to interact with the other group.
- When interaction does take place, it serves to reinforce stereotypes.
- The climate in the group becomes more formal and there is a focus on tasks.
- Leadership of the group becomes more autocratic.
- The need to present a 'united front' means that the group becomes highly structured and organised.

Many of these characteristics can also be seen in individuals who compete against each other to get their proposals accepted.

Negotiation is a skill that is helpful if you wish to influence others effectively. One technology leader with whom my organisation worked, was responsible for implementation of a multinational technology-change programme.. To gain buy-in to the programme, he needed to recognise the power bases within the organisation and negotiate effectively with the key influencers.

To negotiate well requires mutual respect and an understanding of the principles of 'give' and 'get'.

Stages of negotiation

There are six steps in negotiation:

1. Preparation.
2. Opening the discussion.
3. Stating objectives.
4. Testing issues.
5. Reassessing.
6. Agreement.

Preparation

Most people do not spend sufficient time preparing for negotiation. During the preparation phase it is helpful to:

Plan:

- Define objectives: Be clear about exactly what you want from the negotiation and what you need to get to receive your needs.
- Decide what you are willing to concede to get what you want.
- Write down what you think the other party's objectives may be.
- What do they want to get and what could they give in return?

Clarify the issues:

- What is the rationale behind your objectives?
- What is the supporting framework for your position?
- What is the best way to present this to the other party?
- What is likely to be the other party's position?
- How will they support this?

- What are the key differences between your position and the other party's?

Gather information

It is essential to find out as much as possible about the person you will be negotiating with:

- What is their power base?
- What do they need?
- What personal power do you have that can be used positively and constructively during the negotiation?

Develop a strategy for achieving your and the other person's objectives. How will you conduct the negotiation? What is the best approach to take?

Establish tactics for:

- Building relationships and setting the climate. How can you best establish rapport with the other person?
- Dealing with conflict: what will be the points of conflict? How will you deal with them?
- Resolution of issues: how will you attempt to resolve the conflict? What concessions are you prepared to make and when?
- Agreement: what should the agreement process be? Should this be formal or informal?

Opening the discussion

Your preparation will help you think through the best approach to take in opening the discussion. It is good to create a relaxed, informal atmosphere. Ask questions to find out more about the other person.

Stating objectives

Find out from the other person what they want and need from the outcome of the negotiation. State what you want and need.

Testing issues

Use hypothetical questions to assess what the other party is prepared to give and what they want in return. 'What ifs' and 'How would you feel if' are useful means of testing what concessions might be made.

Reassessing

If there is a difference of viewpoint or disagreement, the best tactic is to:

- Listen;
- Ask questions;
- Go back over the areas of agreement;
- Take stock;
- Restate your case;
- Be creative – brainstorm possible strategies; and
- Solve problems jointly.

You may nevertheless encounter someone who won't give in. In which case, avoid the impulse to lose your cool:

- Persevere;
- Listen;

- Ask variations of questions;
- Seek areas of agreement; and
- Explore alternatives.

Agreement

There are some simple rules about reaching agreement in a negotiation:

- If you are not sure, don't close the discussion.
- When you are sure, close.

The temptation is to ignore important issues simply to reach the close.

A useful tip is to try to reach agreement at each stage of the negotiation so that there are things you both agree to as you go along. This is called 'an agreement staircase' and leads to a final joint outcome. So, for example, you may say: *"So far, we've agreed that the issue needs to be investigated in more detail and we will both provide someone from each of our teams to do this."*

Remember also to confirm what has finally been agreed so there can be no going back.

Critical mistakes in negotiating

Expert negotiators cite six critical mistakes that lead to stalemate or negotiations breaking down:

1. **Lack of preparation.** Preparation allows you to consider what you and the other party need. It provides a good picture of your options and tactics.

2. **Seeing negotiation as win/lose.** Each party needs to conclude the negotiation feeling something has been gained. If you approach a negotiation thinking that you are going to 'win', confrontation is sure to ensue.

3. **Use of aggressive behaviour.** Research shows that aggressive behaviour such as arguing, loss of temper and name-calling leads to resistance in the other party. Assertiveness rather than aggression makes for a more effective outcome.

4. **Talking too much**. People who talk too much in a negotiation do not create a cooperative atmosphere. Listening is a powerful way of finding out more about the other person's needs and concerns.

5. **Ignoring conflict.** Conflict is bound to occur in negotiation. The temptation is to avoid the issues. However, in pushing them under the carpet, you do not move closer to agreement.

6. **Impatience.** Negotiations are often not concluded in one meeting. Ideas and proposals need time to gestate. A hurried agreement may mean that both parties do not get what they need.

Assess your negotiation style

Use the questionnaire below to identify the behaviours you rely upon most in negotiations where:

- 0 = Never;
- 1 = Rarely;
- 2 = Sometimes;

- 3 = Occasionally;
- 4 = Frequently; and
- 5 = Always.

Table 13: Negotiation Style Self-Assessment Questionnaire

Statement	Your score out of 5
1. I find conflict stressful and avoid it at all costs.	
2. I express my views directly.	
3. I concede my point to restore harmony.	
4. I believe in give and take.	
5. I seek a solution that everyone will be happy with.	
6. I prefer to delay discussing an issue until I gather more accurate information.	
7. I prefer quick, decisive action and do not have	

Statement	Your score out of 5
time for lengthy negotiations.	
8. I care more about maintaining my personal relationship than the issue.	
9. I am willing to go part way on an issue if it is only moderately important to me.	
10. I stand up for my own interests and needs while honoring the interests and needs of others.	
11. I tend to avoid an issue when I feel I have no power to change the situation.	
12. I believe part of my job is to enforce unpopular rules and ensure compliance.	
13. I believe my views are less important than those of others.	

Statement	Your score out of 5
14. I aim to find a fair mixture of gains and losses for both parties.	
15. I seek a satisfactory outcome for both me and others.	
16. I prefer not to voice my opinions as I believe the damage incurred would outstrip the benefits.	
17. I am not open to hearing others' point of views.	
18. I prefer to please others and may overextend myself to do so.	
19. I try to find compromise solutions.	
20. I aim at consensus-building through a win-win negotiation.	

Statement	Your score out of 5
21. I wait to uncover the real issue and choose my battles wisely.	
22. People may describe me as impatient, insensitive and detached.	
23. I tend to soften what I say so as not to hurt people's feelings.	
24. I aim for the middle ground.	
25. I tell the other person my ideas and ask for theirs in return.	

Now transfer your scores to the following grid. Then total your scores for each column.

Table 14: Negotiation-styles Questionnaire

Your score for Avoiding:	Your Score for Competing:	Your score for Accommodating:	Your score for Compromising:	Your score for Collaborating:
Q1	Q2	Q3	Q4	Q5
Q6	Q7	Q8	Q9	Q10
Q11	Q12	Q13	Q14	Q15
Q16	Q17	Q18	Q19	Q20
Q21	Q22	Q23	Q24	Q25
Total score for Avoiding:	Total score for Competing:	Total score for Accommodating:	Total score for Compromising:	Total score for Collaborating:

Interpreting your scores

Your scores show your preferences for each of the five negotiation behaviours:

- Avoiding.
- Competing.
- Accommodating.
- Compromising.
- Collaborating.

A score of 5 to 10 indicates a minor reliance on this style in negotiations, 11 to 19 a moderate reliance, and 20 or more a strong reliance on this behaviour in negotiations.

If you have scored 20 or more in more than one behaviour, this means that you rely on both sets of behaviour when you negotiate, for example you score highest on Competing then Compromising, which means you strive to get your way in negotiations and then if this does not work, you revert to Compromise.

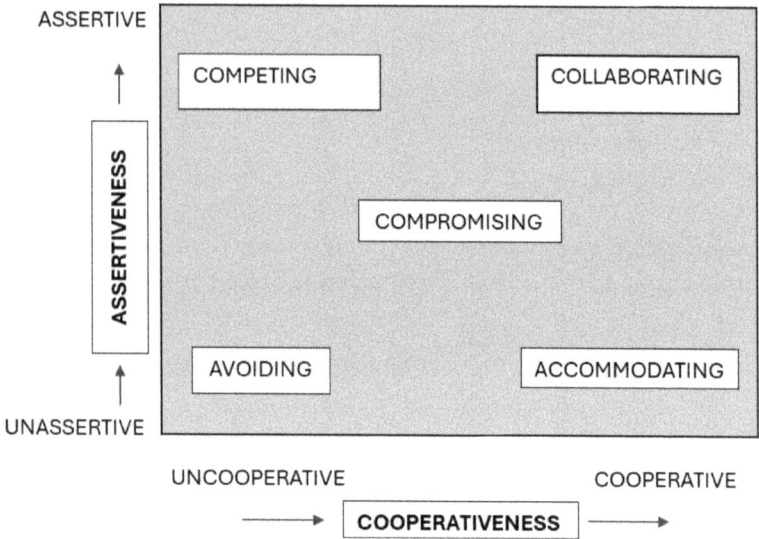

Figure 7: Five Approaches to Negotiation

Five approaches to negotiation

In negotation situations, we can describe a person's behaviour along two dimensions:

1. **Assertiveness:** the extent to which the individual attempts to satisfy their own concerns; and
2. **Cooperativeness:** the extent to which the individual attempts to satisfy the other person's concerns.

These two dimensions of behaviour can be used to define five specific methods for negotiating:

- *Avoiding* is a set of behaviours that is unassertive and uncooperative. This is when the negotiator avoids confrontation. Avoiding might take the form of side-stepping an issue, delaying addressing an issue until a better time, or simply withdrawing from a negotiation. At worst, it results in a lose-lose situation where both results and relationships are put at risk.

- *Competing* is a win-lose approach. It is assertive and uncooperative. This is where the negotiator focuses exclusively on their own objectives at the other person's expense. It is a short-term approach where trust and relationships are discarded in pursuit of the negotiator's desire to be powerful and win.

- *Accommodating* is where the negotiator puts emphasis on the needs and wants of others while ignoring their own wants and needs. It is a lose-win approach that is unassertive and cooperative. The accommodating negotiator concedes in the hope of maintaining harmony and good relationships.

- *Compromising* is a common approach to negotiation. It is a half-way house in both assertiveness and cooperation and not totally win-win. Why is this? Compromising falls on a middle ground between competing and accommodating. It results in getting some of what the negotiator wants but at the same time making concessions, splitting the difference.

- *Collaborating* is a true win-win solution – both assertive and cooperative. It goes beyond compromising as the negotiator seeks to work with the other person to find a solution that fully satisfies the concerns of both parties. Collaborating often involves working jointly with the other person to understand each other's point of view and finding creative solutions that satisfy both parties.

It is generally acknowledged that a compromising and/or collaborating approach to negotiations brings greater win-win outcomes, sustains trust and encourages long-term relationships.

> Carol went to see the HR director to explain the insider risk management programme and to try to make a coalition with him to support the project. During the discussion, it became clear that in return for his support, the HR director wished for more engagement from members of the IT team in a change management programme that the HR director was sponsoring. Having stated her objectives, Carol listened to the HR director's needs, and together the two parties and Carol's manager negotiated a collaborative agreement of mutual support.

Takeaways from this chapter

1. To negotiate well requires mutual respect and an understanding of the principles of give and get.
2. There are six steps in negotiation:
   - Preparation.
   - Opening the discussion.
   - Stating objectives.
   - Testing issues.
   - Reassessing.

- Agreement.

3. When negotiating, people can take one of five different approaches: Avoiding, Competing, Accommodating, Compromising, Collaborating.

CHAPTER 9: DEALING WITH DIFFICULT SITUATIONS

When we try to influence and persuade others, the reality is that at times we will encounter difficult situations. In this chapter, we discuss:

- The different approaches people take to difficult situations; and
- Methods for managing conflict and disaccord.

When we fail to influence effectively, conflict and disagreement can happen.

> Our cyber security expert Carol found herself in conflict with the head of the legal department for not having consulted with them before presenting her proposal to the senior leadership team. The head of the legal team believed that the proposed programme did not put enough emphasis on the legal consequences of insider risk management. Carol believed strongly that the proposal did take this into account.
>
> The head of the legal team took an aggressive stance and told Carol he would block the proposal.

The different approaches people take to conflict

As we've seen from the last chapter on negotiation, there are five different ways that people can deal with conflict.

Many people back away from discord, wary of the problems it may cause. This reluctance may lead to avoidance of potential problem areas or suppression of disagreement. I recently worked with an IT manager and her team to help confront the behaviour of two team members whose clashes were having a negative impact on the service the team provided. Other team members were, of course, aware of the problem, and had been for some time but no one was willing to confront the issue in case they, too, became embroiled. However, denial doesn't mean conflict goes away and it may get worse.

The other side to this is that some people relish conflict. The late Robert Maxwell was said to welcome a battle, haranguing people in meetings and threatening them. Some people may deliberately adopt this stance to get their own way.

Avoidance and aggression are not the only ways in which people react to conflict. As we've seen, unassertive people give in and unwillingly collaborate with the other person. This may lead to an apparent resumption of normal working relationships but often at the expense of one person's self-esteem.

In many cases, it pays to take a different stance and adopt a win-win approach by trying to reach a compromise with the person. For example, a manager, let's say of the IT team, may agree to take on additional administrative workload from another department if, in turn, that department is prepared to help them out when they are busy. By its very win-win nature, compromise involves give and take.

Research shows that few people adopt a truly collaborative approach to finding a solution that fully satisfies the needs of both parties; it requires constructive building of common ground that starts off with thorough understanding on both sides. In our example, is the IT team the best department to take over the administration? Why has the need arisen in the first place? When are the busy peaks in the department? Is the other department acting as backup the best use of resource? What are the options? These questions can help form the basis of a lasting agreement.

Research backs up that more constructive and supportive behaviours towards customers and colleagues is a lot more effective than merely flatly stating obstacles and difficulties, which can drive people into corners they find difficult to back out of. And it leaves the problem unresolved.

Practical steps to handling conflict

My top tips for managing difficult situations are below:

- Firstly, understand how you typically respond to conflict. Practise being flexible and putting yourself in the other person's shoes.
- Listen carefully to words and feelings.
- Reflect back what has been said/felt to build greater respect and shared understanding.
- Be clear on your case but don't become so fixated by your point of view that you get tunnel vision on other perspectives.

- Be prepared to negotiate where necessary to reach an agreement that is acceptable to both parties in the long-term as well as immediately.
- Review your own behaviours and the implications of major decisions on other people. Ask for feedback on how you handle conflict and set yourself some improvement goals.
- Communicate regularly and build relationships, even or especially when damage has been caused.

Helpful phrases when handling conflict

Remaining calm and assertive while acknowledging and respecting the views of others is a key skill when managing difficult situations. Here are some phrases that allow you to do this:

- *"I have a different take on that than you. Would you like to hear my thoughts?"*
- *"Help me understand your point of view."*
- *"Where are you coming from with this?"*
- *"If I understand you correctly, you mean/you felt..."*
- *"Can I just check I have understood? Feel free to correct me if I'm wrong."*
- *"So, if I understand you right, you interpreted X in X way? Is that right?"*
- *"Tell me how I have not understood you."*
- *"Sounds like what I said didn't get received by you how I intended – would you let me try again?"*
- *"I am aware that I did not handle the feedback well."*

- *"I am concerned. You say you understand but your body language suggests that you may not...is there anything you would like us to revisit?"*
- *"Is it OK if we move on now to work out how we want to move forward?"*
- *"I'm ready to look for solutions if you are?"*

> Carol went to see the head of the legal team and addressed their differences in a calm and assertive manner. She made sure she listened actively to what he had to say and that she showed that she understood his point of view. She then explained how the proposed programme already addressed most of the issues that the legal head had raised. She asked for his input on how to move forward and how they could jointly look for solutions, in this way winning his support.

Takeaways from this chapter

1. Part of being an effective influencer is knowing how to handle difficult situations.
2. This requires a calm and mature approach, assertiveness as well as the ability to listen and understand the other person's point of view.

CHAPTER 10: SUMMARY AND ACTION PLANNING

Key learning points

In this book, we've looked at the following:

- The need to be self-aware to be able to influence effectively.
- The four personality styles: Amiable, Expressive, Direct and Analytical, and the need to flex your own style to better persuade others. Gaining feedback can help you to better understand your own impact.
- The importance of being assertive and for your words, tone and body language to be congruent.
- Push and Pull language and how a balance of both types of influence behaviours leads to successful outcomes.
- Tips and activities to help increase your self-confidence.
- Increasing your self-awareness to better understand others and adapt accordingly. In the chapter on sources of power, I stressed that referent, expert, information and legitimate power have the most beneficial impact when we try to persuade others.
- The process for getting your voice heard and different influence strategies you can apply including logical facts, pros and cons, big-picture, and participative.

- Tactics you can adopt to deal with Cynics, Spectators and Victims.
- Negotiation skills and the five different approaches we can take to manage conflict.
- The need for a calm and assertive approach to difficult situations, seeking compromise and/or collaboration.

In becoming more self-aware and recognising the preferences of others, Carol, the subject matter expert in our continuing example, was able to develop strategies for better influencing the senior management team. She worked on her assertiveness and self-confidence, identified her and the senior managers' sources of power, used a pros and cons strategy for her presentation, demonstrating her expertise. She also built a coalition with the HR director to gain support for her proposal in return for becoming more involved with his change management programme. She dealt effectively with a conflict that arose with the head of the legal team to arrive at a collaborative outcome.

The result of Carol's SOS (Self, Others, Strategy) approach was that she gained unanimous approval from the senior leadership team for the insider risk management programme.

Actions you can take

At the end of the first chapter, I asked you to select a situation (either current or in the past) where you would like /would have liked to influence others more effectively.

Look back over your notes and reflections as you undertook the exercises and activities in this book. What have you learned that can help you more effectively influence in this situation?

I invite you to then list the tips and actions you can take forward to become a better influencer.

Write your top three actions in the box below:

Top 3 actions:
1.
2.
3.

To ensure you become more effective, prioritise action one and take it first. Think through how you will do this, and when and who you need for support.

I hope that you've found this book useful and that it's helped increase your influencing skills.

FURTHER READING

IT Governance Publishing (ITGP) is the world's leading publisher for governance and compliance. Our industry-leading pocket guides, books and training resources are written by real-world practitioners and thought leaders. They are used globally by audiences of all levels, from students to C-suite executives.

Our high-quality publications cover all IT governance, risk and compliance frameworks and are available in a range of formats. This ensures our customers can access the information they need in the way they need it.

Our other soft skills publications include:

- *Well-being in the Workplace –A guide to resilience for individuals and teams* by Sarah Cook, *www.itgovernance.co.uk/shop/product/well-being-in-the-workplace-a-guide-to-resilience-for-individuals-and-teams*
- *Making a Success of Managing and Working Remotely* by Sarah Cook, *www.itgovernance.co.uk/shop/product/making-a-success-of-managing-and-working-remotely*
- *Building a High-Performance Team – Proven techniques for effective team working* by Sarah Cook, *https://www.itgovernance.co.uk/shop/product/building-a-high-performance-team*

- *Changing how you manage and communicate change – Focusing on the human side of change* by Naomi Karten, *https://www.itgovernance.co.uk/shop/product/effectiv e-career-development-advice-for-establishing-an-enjoyable-career*

For more information on ITGP and branded publishing services, and to view our full list of publications, visit *www.itgovernancepublishing.co.uk*.

To receive regular updates from ITGP, including information on new publications in your area(s) of interest, sign up for our newsletter:

www.itgovernancepublishing.co.uk/topic/newsletter.

Branded publishing

Through our branded publishing service, you can customise ITGP publications with your company's branding.

Find out more at

www.itgovernancepublishing.co.uk/topic/branded-publishing-services.

Related services

ITGP is part of GRC International Group, which offers a comprehensive range of complementary products and services to help organisations meet their objectives.

For a full range of GCR International Group's resources, visit *www.itgovernance.co.uk/*.

Training services

The IT Governance training programme is built on our extensive practical experience designing and implementing management systems based on ISO standards, best practice and regulations.

Our courses help attendees develop practical skills and comply with contractual and regulatory requirements. They also support career development via recognised qualifications.

Learn more about our training courses and view the full course catalogue at *www.itgovernance.co.uk/training*.

Professional services and consultancy

We are a leading global consultancy of IT governance, risk management and compliance solutions. We advise businesses around the world on their most critical issues and present cost-saving and risk-reducing solutions based on international best practice and frameworks.

We offer a wide range of delivery methods to suit all budgets, timescales and preferred project approaches.

Find out how our consultancy services can help your organisation at *www.itgovernance.co.uk/consulting*.

Industry news

Want to stay up to date with the latest developments and resources in the IT governance and compliance market? Subscribe to our Weekly Round-up newsletter and we will send you mobile-friendly emails with fresh news and features about your preferred areas of interest, as well as unmissable offers and free resources to help you successfully start your projects. _www.itgovernance.co.uk/weekly-round-up_.

EU for product safety is Stephen Evans, The Mill Enterprise Hub, Stagreenan, Drogheda, Co. Louth, A92 CD3D, Ireland. (servicecentre@itgovernance.eu)

www.ingramcontent.com/pod-product-compliance
Lightning Source LLC
Chambersburg PA
CBHW042315210326
41599CB00038B/7132